Anna M. Scott

The U. S. C., Cook Book

Compiled for the Universalist Social Circle of Junction City, Kas.

Anna M. Scott

The U. S. C., Cook Book
Compiled for the Universalist Social Circle of Junction City, Kas.

ISBN/EAN: 9783744799256

Printed in Europe, USA, Canada, Australia, Japan

Cover: Foto ©Lupo / pixelio.de

More available books at **www.hansebooks.com**

TX715
.S425

◣THE U. S. C.,

GOOK BOOK,

COMPILED FOR THE

UNIVERSALIST ✢ SOCIAL ✢ CIRCLE,

OF

JUNCTION CITY, KAS.

PRICE 25 CENTS.

BY

ANNA M. SCOTT.

WHAT THE COOK BOOK DID FOR PADDY.

I.

W HIN I axed ye to marry, Norah Machree,
    Ye turned yer swate head, with a quare little
      look ;
      " 'Tis a weary long while ye'll be waitin' for me,
For I'm never to wed till I've learned how to cook.
      Says me mither, says she,
      Sure Norah Machree,
Ye may sing like an angel and talk like a book,
    But ye niver shall wed till ye larn how to cook ! "

II.

"That's aisy," says I ; tache a pig how to squale !
    There's nuthin ' at all to be doin' but this :
Jist hang on the kittle and shtir in the male,
    And betwane ivery mouthful look out for a kiss !
      Says me mither, says she,
      " Wed Norah Machree ; "
And fax ! I'll obey her ; tis little I'll miss,
    If betwane ivery mouthful you give me a kiss ! "

III.

Be jabers ! ye fetched me a box on the head !
    Here's yer pay for that same ! tis 'the latest cook book.
Last avenin' I shpake to your mither instead, —
    Ye'd better make haste and be larnin' to cook :
      For yer mither, says she,
      " Thrust Norah Machree ;
And she shook her ould head wid a terrible look :
    " I'll wollop the girl till she larns how to cook !

IV.

Coom now, rade it all ! ye can rade like the sphinx.
    May the ladies be blest for complatin' me bliss !
Shtir the bride cake me dove ; 'twill be aisy as winks,
    And as light as me heart, while ye give me a kiss.
      Says me mither, says she,
      " Bring Norah Machree ;
We've a cow and thray pigs, and 'tis little she'll miss ;
    If betwane ivery mouthful ye give her a kiss."

DEDICATION.
—:o:—

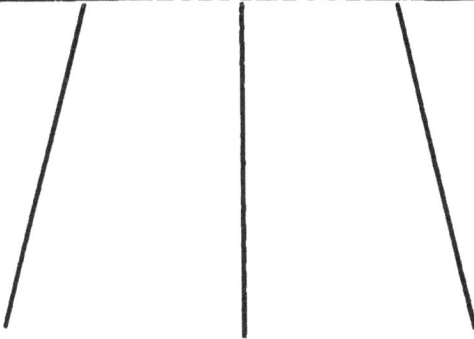

To Mrs. Sarah M Barnes, the faithful and efficient leader in our church work, this little book is affectionately dedicated. ☆

Though humble in aspect, may it suggest the heart-felt appreciation of her labors in the U. S. C., and the regard of her sincere friend, the author.

ANNA M. SCOTT.

INTRODUCTION.

AT a certain luncheon party, our hostess, Mrs. Smith, being complimented upon the excellence of her viands, took occasion to give us some of her early experience in cooking

"Soon after our marriage," said she, "My husband met with crushing losses in business, and in consequence was greatly depressed in spirits. With true loyalty to our business firm, I hailed the opportunity to show my heroism as a good, economical wife. I resolved on sudden retrenchment in household expenses. One item had troubled me from the first. Our housekeeper was wasteful and careless. Her miserable cooking had kept my husband longing for his mother's old fashioned living. This added, I knew, to his gloominess; for I never found anyone so dependent as Mr. Smith on having just what he wanted to eat. An inspiration seized me It was the hope of snatching my husband from ruin. I determined he should have some of his favorite dishes every day. This would revive his spirits and turn the financial scale. To this end I turned off the cook, and resolved that very day to give Mr. Smith some of his favorite peach pie.

"I went to the kitchen in search of the old receipt book. Alas! it was gone. The cook had taken her own, for as I remembered I had given her the book Without repining, I rallied to meet the situation I could make pies without a receipt book. Of course I could I had seen my mother-in-law cook everything. Let's see! Peach pie? It is not peach season Apple pie? That is nice, and here are dried apples. How white and beautiful! What delicious pie they will make. In a jiffy the crust was rolled and laid smoothly, then the rings of white evaporated apples spread carefully. then a coating of sugar with flour dredged over it. I was almost sure this was mother's formula before putting on the top crust. Full of confidence the pie went into the oven. I served it at dinner with due formality. But to my chagrin, the pie was so tough and hard that it could not be eaten at all. Now as if the fates had planned a climax to my mortification, who do you suppose dropped in just at the hour of this unfortunate dinner? My mother-in-law! And when I told her of the dried apples placed between crusts without being first cooked, she laughed till the tears rolled down her cheeks.

"That apple pie incident remains a standing joke in our family yet. But I came out victorious at last, and it was by getting hold of a good cook book. One gotten up by Kansas women, who are scientific cooks."

In the receipts which this U. S. C. Cook Book contains, there is nothing but what has been tried by persons whose names are appended. Each one has been tested at home, where the substantial dishes as well as the delicacies have been enjoyed. The excellence of many of the viands has become known to the public through various social channels when banquets and entertainments were given. After such occasions noted successes are referred to as Mrs. J. C. Scott's pie crust, Mrs Baskin's white citron cake, or Mrs. Crail's graham pudding. etc , etc.

Many wishing to know how such and such favorites were prepared, have asked for various receipts. This evident demand for practical directions has suggested their publication in the pages that follow. Doubtless an appreciative public will readily discover that much pains has been taken to collect and arrange this useful information, and will extend liberal patronage as a just reward.

Note how minutely the necessary details are given in regard to preparation of ingredients as also quantity and kind. Read, if you please, as a specimen, the receipt for "chow chow" in the pickle department. The directions are so explicit in this little book that if well followed there is no chance for blunder, such as the pie story illustrates.

M. P. Davis.

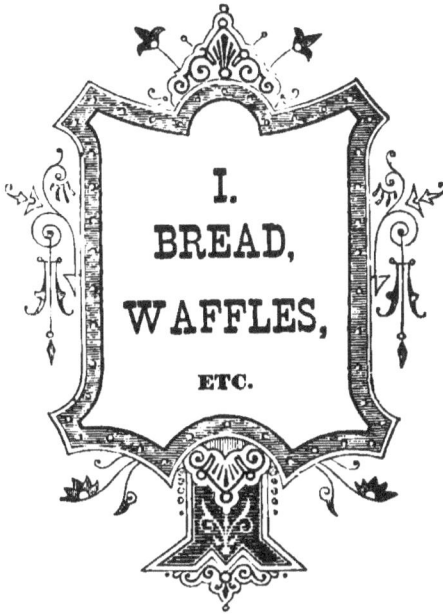

I.

BREAD,

WAFFLES,

ETC.

1   HOP AND POTATO YEAST.

6 large potatoes.

3 quarts boiling water.

1 cup hops.

2 tablespoonfuls salt.

2 tablespoonfuls sugar.

1 cup yeast

Pare potatoes and put them in a stew pan with the hops tied loosely in a thin muslin bag, and the boiling water. Cook one half hour, r move the potatoes with a skimmer and mash them in a large bowl till fine and light. Pour upon them the water in which they were boiled, add sugar and salt Rub this mixture through a seive and let it stand until blood warm (98°) then stir in yeast and cover closely; set in a warm place (temperature 75°) to rise This will require about six hours. Put in air tight glass jars and set in a cool place It will keep for three weeks. Use porcelain or granite kettle. This will make three quarts.

ANON.

2   YEAST BREAD.

For four large or six medium sized loaves use —

1 quart boiling water.

3 large potatoes, pared.

¾ cup yeast

1 tablespoonful salt.

3½ quarts flour.

Cook potatoes in the boiling water half an hour; mash fine; pour over them the boiling water; let stand until blood warm (98°). Add yeast and three quarts of flour, beating it in with a spoon; cover and let rise over night. In the morning beat in the salt and half of the remaining flour; use remnant of flour for kneading on the board. Knead for twenty minutes or one-half hour. Put dough back into the bowl and cover. Let it rise to double its size. Shape into loaves and let them rise to double their original size. Bake one hour in a moderate oven.

The addition of a tablespoonful of sugar and two or three of lard or butter, improves the bread. ANON.

3 "WHEAT AND INDIAN" BREAD.

When making wheat bread reserve some of the sponge.

Take one quart of boiling water and a little salt—thicken with corn meal as for mush—let cool.

Take pan of flour hollowed in center; put in the mush and one pint of N. O. molasses; then add wheat bread sponge, a little salt and two spoonfuls melted lard. Mix stiff; let rise; mould into loaves.

Bake slowly for one hour or more.

MRS. JOSEPHINE BLAKELY.

4 BREAD.

1 cake compressed yeast ($\frac{1}{2}$ oz.)

1 pint of water to which a little salt has been added.

Knead in all the flour it will take.

Let rise three hours in 75° heat—mould in loaves—rise one hour—bake as usual. MRS J. W. BARNEY.

5 CORN BREAD.

$\frac{3}{4}$ quart corn meal.

$\frac{3}{4}$ quart sweet milk.

3 teaspoonfuls baking powder.

$\frac{1}{2}$ cup sugar,

3 eggs—salt—3 cups (cool) boiled rice

MRS R. M. CRAIL.

6 COFFEE BREAD.

2 cups sugar.
2 cups sweet milk.
1 small cup butter.
3 teaspoonfuls baking powder.
4 eggs.
1 cup currants or two teaspoonfuls cinnamon. Enough flour to make quite stiff   MRS. R M. CRAIL.

7 MUFFINS.

2 eggs.
2 large spoonfuls sugar.
2 cups flour.
2 cups sweet milk.
2 teaspoonfuls melted butter.
3 teaspoonfuls baking powder.
Salt to taste.   MRS. R M CRAIL.

8 BROWN BREAD.

1 quart water.
2 cups flour.
4 cups corn meal.
1 cup molasses.
1 teaspoonful soda   Steam   MRS A. P. TROTT.

9 BROWN BREAD.

1 quart corn meal.
1 pint graham flour.
1 quart milk—sweet.
1 cup molasses
1 teaspoonful soda   Steam.   MRS D. N. HICKS.

10   INDIAN CAKES.

1 pint sour milk.

1 beaten egg.

1 small tablespoonful brown sugar.

1 teaspoonful salt.

Stir in a mixture of two parts Indian meal and one part wheat flour until you have a stiff batter. Add a small teaspoonful of soda dissolved in a little hot water. Thin to the proper consistency with sweet milk.

Bake on a hot griddle.   ANON.

11   POP OVERS.

3 cups milk.

3 cups flour.

3 eggs.

Mix and add one tablespoonful melted butter and pinch of salt.

Fry in hot lard.   MRS. C. W. BABBAGE.

12   WAFFLES.

1 pint sour milk.

½ cup shortening.

1 teaspoonful soda

1 egg.

Salt.

Flour to make a stiff batter.   MRS C. W. BABBAGE.

II.

MEATS.

13 BEEF COLLOPS.

Use—

1 quart cold roast beef, chopped very fine.

2 tablespoonfuls flour.

4 tablespoonfuls butter.

1 teaspoonful chopped onion.

½ teaspoonful chopped parsley.

2 teaspoonfuls salt.

¼ teaspoonful pepper.

½ pint stock made of the bones and hard bits of roast beef.

Put butter on the stove, and when it gets hot add the onion and parsley. Cook until the onion turns a light brown, then add flour and stir until smooth Next add stock and cook two minutes, then add meat, salt and pepper and stir thoroughly. Cover the pan and cook slowly for twenty minutes. Turn out on a hot dish and garnish with small slices of toast or parsley. Cold steak or raw beef chopped fine may be used for collops. When uncooked beef is taken the cooking should be continued only five minutes after the meat is put with the sauce. **Anon.**

14 TIMBALE OF COLD MEAT.

For six persons use—

1½ pints cold meat chopped fine.

1 level tablespoonful salt.

½ teaspoonful pepper.

½ teaspoonful onion juice.

1 teaspoonful chopped parsley.

1 cup of stock or milk.

2 eggs.

2 tablespoonfuls butter.

½ cup grated bread crumbs.

Mix the seasoning and bread crumbs with the meat. Heat the stock and melt the butter in it, then add the stock

and the two eggs well beaten to the meat, mix thoroughly
and put into a well buttered mould or bowl. Place this in
a pan of warm water and cover with a piece of buttered
paper. Cook for an hour in a moderate oven, and after
turning out on a warm dish, pour brown sauce around it.

ANON.

15   BROWN SAUCE.

Heat three tablespoonfuls of butter in a frying pan.
When it begins to turn brown, add two tablespoonfuls flour,
stir until it becomes dark brown, then draw the pan back to
a cooler place and gradually pour into it one cup and a half
of stock or milk. Stir until it boils, then let it simmer for
three minutes. Season with

½ teaspoonful salt.
¼ teaspoonful pepper.
1 tablespoonful tomato catsup.   ANON.

16   VEAL LOAF.

3 ℔ veal.
¾ ℔ salt pork.
1 cup rolled crackers.
2 eggs.
1 teaspoonful sugar.
4 teaspoonfuls salt.
2 teaspoonfuls pepper.
Make in loaf and bake two hours

MRS. D. N. HICKS.

17   HAM SALAD.

Chop cold boiled ham and cabbage together—more
cabbage than ham—and pour over it dressing same as for
potato salad.   MRS. R. M. CRAIL.

18   HAM PIE.

Slice raw potatoes very thin. Put in a baking dish a layer of the potatoes with bits of butter, pepper, salt and small pieces of raw ham, also cut thin. Over this dredge some flour. Continue in same manner until the dish is filled. Put in sweet milk until you can see it. Cover and bake. When nearly done, remove cover and brown.

MRS. J. C. SCOTT.

19   CECILS.

1 pint meat, chopped fine.

1 tablespoonful butter.

2 tablespoonfuls bread crumbs.

1 tablespoonful chopped parsley.

1 teaspoonful salt.

½ teaspoonful pepper.

1 egg.

Mix meal, butter, salt and pepper together. Put on fire and heat. Remove and add parsley. Beat the egg without separating. Add to it one tablespoonful water.

Make into balls. Dip in egg, then in bread crumbs and fry in smoking hot fat.   LOUISE BARNES.

20   OYSTER PATTIES.

Line patty-pans with good paste. Cut covers to the pans and bake them on sheets of tin.

Wash one quart of oysters out of the liquor and put them into a sauce pan. Add butter size of an egg; one-half teaspoonful mace, juice of one lemon and very little flour. Give them one scald, stirring all the time. Fill the patties; put on the top crust and serve immediately.

This is a nice dish for company, as the crusts can be baked the day before.   MRS. J. C. SCOTT.

21   CROQUETTES.

1 cup chopped meat.

1 cup hot boiled rice.

1 egg.

Season to taste.

Break egg into the rice. Mix with meat and roll in egg and bread crumbs.

Fry in hot lard.   DAISY McCLURE.

22   CORN OYSTERS.

1 pint grated green corn.

1 egg, well beaten.

1 small cup flour.

½ cup butter.

Salt and pepper to taste.

Add a pinch of baking powder to flour.

Fry on a griddle with butter.   MRS. J. C. SCOTT.

23   NOODLE SOUP.

Break a large egg into a bowl and beat into it a little more than half a cup of flour and one-fourth teaspoonful salt.

Work this dough with the hands until it becomes smooth and like putty.

Sprinkle a moulding board with flour, and roll the dough as thin as possible. Let it lie upon the board five minutes, then roll it up loosely and with a sharp knife cut it it into slices about one-third of an inch thick. Spread these little pieces on the board and let them dry for one-half hour. Put on the stove a large sauce pan containing two quarts boiling water. Add a tablespoonful salt, and after turning the noodles into the water cook rapidly twenty-five minutes. Turn into a colander and drain.

ANON.

24   SOUP.

3 pints milk.

3 tablespoonfuls flour.

3 teaspoonfuls salt.

⅛ teaspoonful pepper.

A slice of onion.

A bit of mace

Reserve a half cup of the milk and put the rest with the onion and mace on the stove in a double boiler Mix the flour and cold milk and stir the mixture into the boiling milk. Add the salt and pepper and cook fifteen minutes At the end of that time take out the mace and onion and add the noodles.

Cook five minutes   MRS. J. COPLEY.

25   WHITE SAUCE.

This is an excellent sauce for boiled salt fish.

1 pint milk.

1 pint cream.

4 tablespoonfuls flour.

2 whole eggs.

6 yolks.

Salt and pepper.

Reserve a cup of the milk Place the remainder with the cream in a double boiler. Pour half the cup of milk upon the flour. Stir until smooth. Add the remainder of the milk and stir this into the milk and cream while boiling. Stir the sauce for two minutes Cover and cook for eight minutes longer. Season. Beat the yolks of the eggs with four tablespoonfuls milk. Stir into the sauce and remove from the fire. A tablespoonful of chopped parsley may be added. Boil the two eggs hard. Slice or chop and lay around fish Pour the dressing over whole.

MRS L. S. SARGENT.

26,   '   HOW TO CLEAN CHICKEN.

Singe the chicken. Cut off the head and feet. Remove the oil sack. Cut the skin down the back of the neck. Draw the skin from the neck Separate the windpipe and crop from the skin. Cut it off as far down as possible. Make a vent below the breast bone. Insert the fingers and loosen all the organs in the chicken. Take hold of the gizzard, and draw them all out at once. Cut around the end of intestine and remove it. Wash the chicken carefully and truss it. Bake it fifteen minutes to the pound.

L. B.

III.

EGGS.

27 LYONAISE EGGS.

½ dozen eggs.

2 tablespoonfuls butter.

1 tablespoonful flour.

1 tablespoonful chopped onion.

3 gills milk.

½ teaspoonful salt.

¼ teaspoonful pepper.

½ cup grated bread crumbs.

Cook butter and onion slowly for ten minutes; add flour; cook until smooth, gradually add milk and cook three minutes, stirring during the first minute Add salt and pepper; pour sauce in a deep plate that has been heated. Carefully break the eggs into this plate, cover with the bread crumbs, place in a moderately hot oven, cook four minutes. Serve the eggs in the dish in which they are cooked.

If the flavor of onion is too strong the sauce may be strained, keeping back the bits of onion.   ANON.

28 CURRIED EGGS.

½ dozen hard boiled eggs.

1 cup stock.

½ cup cream or milk.

1 teaspoonful chopped onion.

3 tablespoonfuls butter.

1 tablespoonful flour.

1 teaspoonful curry powder.

Salt and pepper to taste.

Cook onion and butter in a small frying pan for three minutes. Put in flour and curry powder; stir the liquid until it becomes smooth; add the stock and milk and some seasoning and cook for ten minutes. Quarter the eggs, place them in a deep sauce pan, strain the sauce over them and serve very hot with or without toast. More curry powder may be used if one chooses.

MRS. J. COPLEY.

29   DEVILED EGGS.

Peel the shells from a dozen hard boiled eggs, cut half in two and remove yelks.

Pulverize the yelks, add a little butter (soft), salt pepper and mustard to taste, moisten with vinegar and fill empty whites.

Arrange on lettuce leaves, and if any of the filling remains over, it may be made into a dressing which can be poured over the eggs by adding a little vinegar.

Mrs J. C. Scott.

30   BEAUREGARD EGGS.

Cover five eggs with boiling water and boil twenty minutes. Remove the shell, chop the whites fine, press the yelks through a fine sieve, but do not mix them. Scald ½ pint milk, rub together one tablespoonful corn starch and a piece of butter the size of a walnut and add to the scalding milk, add chopped whites, salt and pepper to taste.

Toast five slices of bread and arrange them on a hot dish. Cover with a layer of cream sauce, sprinkle one-half the yelks over the cream, add remaining cream sauce then rest of the yelks.

Louise Barnes.

31   CREAM SAUCE.

Put three tablespoonfuls butter in a frying pan and place on the fire, when the butter is hot add two tablespoonfuls flour, stir until smooth, and add gradually one pint cold milk, stir until it boils, add

1 teaspoonful salt.

½ teaspoonful pepper.

A teaspoonful chopped parsley may be added when this sauce is to be used for fish or potatoes

Anon.

32 ## PLAIN OMELET.

Beat 4 eggs until well broken but not until very light; add to them ½ teaspoonful salt and two tablespoonfuls of milk or water. Put one tablespoonful of butter in the omelet pan, place the pan where it will heat slowly. When it becomes hot draw it forward; when the heat is intense pour in the egg mixture and shake vigorously until the egg begins to thicken. Let the pan rest on the stove for about five seconds, then roll up the omelet. When rolled, brown it; it will take about fifteen seconds for this. Turn out and serve at once. **ANON.**

33 ## BAKED OMELET.

For 6 persons —

6 eggs.
½ cup milk.
1 tablespoonful flour.
1 teaspoonful baking powder.
1 large teaspoonful salt.
1 large tablespoonful butter
Mix the milk and flour.

Beat whites of eggs to a stiff froth. Add salt and yolks of eggs and beat for ½ minute longer. Put the butter in a hot frying pan. Add milk, flour and baking powder to the eggs, and stir quickly. Turn the mixture in the buttered pan. Put the pan in a rather hot oven for ten minutes. At the end of that time fold the omelet and turn out on a warm dish. Serve immediately. **ANON.**

34 ## OMELET SOUFFLE

Whites of 6 eggs.
Yelks of 3 eggs.
3 tablespoonfuls powdered sugar.
Juice of ½ lemon or a teaspoonful of vanilla.

Beat the yelks. Then add the yelks, sugar and flavoring to the whites. Heat in a buttered baking dish. Dust with powdered sugar. Bake fifteen minutes in a quick oven. **LOUISE BARNES.**

IV.

PIES.

35 ## PIE CRUST.

3 cups sifted flour.

1 cup lard.

1 teaspoonful sugar.

1 teaspoonful salt.

⅓ cup cold water.

This is sufficient for three pies.   MRS. J. C. SCOTT.

36 ## BANANA CREAM PIE.

1 quart milk.

1 cup sugar

½ cup butter.

5 eggs.

2½ tablespoonfuls corn starch.

Bananas.   Powdered sugar on top.

Heat milk, add sugar, butter, eggs and corn starch dissolved in a little milk—add the bananas sliced, and bake with one crust.   MRS. R. M. CRAIL

37 ## LEMON PIE.

1 lemon.

2 yelks eggs

2 tablespoonfuls corn starch

1 cup sugar.

Lump butter size of an egg.

1 pint boiling water.

Cook in a double kettle. Bake with one crust. Use whites of eggs for frosting.   MRS. BABBAGE.

38 ## ORANGE SHORT CAKE.

Make a rich crust as for ordinary shortcake and put in sliced oranges sprinkled with sugar.

MRS. W. W. BASKIN.

39   LEMON CREAM PIE.

Juice of 3 lemons and rind of one.

1 teaspoonful butter.

1½ tablespoonful corn starch.

1 large cup water.

1 cup granulated sugar.

4 tablespoonfuls powdered sugar.

4 eggs.

Mix the corn starch with four tablespoonfuls of the water. Put the remainder of the water into a sauce pan with the lemon rind, the lemon juice and the granulated sugar, and heat to the boiling point. Stir the corn starch into the boiling mixture and cook for two minutes. Stir the butter in and set away to cool; when cool add the yelks of the four eggs, well beaten. Pour the mixture into a large deep plate that has been lined with paste, and bake in a moderate oven thirty-five minutes

Beat the whites of the eggs to a stiff froth, add powdered sugar, and cover pie with same. Let it brown in oven. This will make one large or two small pies.

ANON.

40   TRANSPARENT PIE.

Yelks of 8 eggs beaten very light.

2 cups sugar.

1 teaspoonful vanilla.

This will make three pies.

Beat whites to a stiff froth. Sweeten with pulverized sugar, and put on top.   MRS. M. A. WINANS.

41   CRUMB PIE.

Make crust as for ordinary pastry. Line a tin as for custard pie. Take two tablespoonfuls molasses in a cup, add four tablespoonfuls water, a pinch of soda Stir. Put this into the crust For the crumbs take one small cup flour, butter size of egg, one-half cup sugar. Rub with the hands until crumbs are formed. Put on top of the molasses and bake. Nice for breakfast with coffee.

Mrs. W. W. Baskin.

42 BOILED PIE.

Make a good baking powder biscuit dough, and in the bottom of a stew-pan put any kind of fruit apples (preferably). Roll part of the dough and cut it in slices, put a layer over the fruit, then another layer of fruit. Roll out the remainder of the dough, cut a good sized hole in the middle, put over the fruit, and add water enough to about half cover. Cover and boil forty minutes and watch that it does not boil dry.

When done, eat with sugar and cream. Excellent.

Mrs. Mary Irwin, Danville, Iowa.

43 CHEAP MINCE MEAT.

1 cup chopped cooked meat.
2 cups chopped apples.
½ cup chopped raisins.
½ cup currants.
1 cup cider.
½ cup molasses.
1 cup water in which the meat was boiled.
2 teaspoonfuls salt.
1 teaspoonful cinnamon.
1 teaspoonful allspice.
½ teaspoonful cloves.
½ teaspoonful nutmeg.

The cider may be omitted and the juice and rind of a lemon used instead. Mix all together and then heat to the boiling point. Anon.

44   STRAWBERRY SHORT CAKE.

1 cup sugar.

1 cup milk.

1 egg.

1 tablespoonful melted butter.

2½ cups flour.

2 teaspoonfuls baking powder.

Pinch of salt. Mix as for cake. Bake in layers. Split and put berries between layers.

Mrs R. M. Crail.

V.

PUDDINGS.

45 SUET PUDDING.

1 large cup of finely chopped suet.

3 eggs.

1 cup sugar.

1 cup molasses.

1 cup sour milk.

1 teaspoonful soda.

½ cup currants; same of raisins. Flour enough to make rather stiff batter.

Steam three hours. MRS. FLORA B. WINANS.

46 SWEET SAUCE FOR PUDDINGS.

½ cup butter.

1 cup sugar.

1 cup milk.

Stir sugar and butter together to a cream. Boil the milk, and while boiling stir in one teaspoonful cornstarch dissolved in milk. Pour the milk while boiling, over the butter and sugar. MRS. R. M. CRAIL.

47 PINE-APPLE PUDDING.

½ package gelatine.

6 eggs—yelks.

3 cups milk.

1 cup sugar.

3 cups grated pine apple.

Soak gelatine in one-half cup of cold milk for two hours. Then put two cups milk into double boiler on the stove. Beat together sugar, salt and yelks of eggs. Add remaining one-half cup milk. Now stir into the boiling milk the pine-apple, gelatine and egg mixture. Cook four minutes, stirring all the while. Take from the fire and stir in cold water five minutes. Put in a mold. Set in a cold place five or six hours. ANON.

48   GRAHAM PUDDING.

1 cup raisins.

1 cup molasses.

1 teaspoonful soda dissolved in small cup milk.

½ teaspoonful salt.

2 cups graham flour.

Steam two hours.

SAUCE.

1 cup sugar.

½ cup butter.

1 tablespoonful flour.

Cream all together, and add hot water until it is thin enough.   MRS. R. M. CRAIL.

49   STEAMED ROLY-POLY PUDDING.

For six persons use—

1 pint flour.

1 teaspoonful sugar.

½ teaspoonful salt.

2 tablespoonfuls butter.

Nearly a small cup milk.

3 pints berries.

Mix the dry ingredients Rub through a sieve Rub the butter into the mixture. Add milk and stir dough into a smooth ball. Roll to the thickness of one-third of an inch. Spread the berries over the dough, keeping free about an inch at each end and one side Roll up the dough, beginning at the side where the berries reach to the edge. Press together the ends of this roll, then lay the roll in a buttered pan. Cover with a napkin and place in a steamer over a kettle of boiling water. Steam two hours. Serve with a hot rich sauce.

Any kind of fruit may be used for this dessert.

ANON.

50 PEACH AND TAPIOCA PUDDING.

1 can peaches.

½ pint tapioca (generous).

¾ cup sugar.

½ teaspoonful salt.

1 quart water.

Soak the tapioca over night in the cold water. In the morning, turn it with the water into a double boiler and cook one hour. Take from stove. Add salt, sugar and juice of the peaches. Stir thoroughly. Pour one half the mixture in a well-buttered pudding dish. Lay in the peaches. Pour over them the remainder of the tapioca. Bake one hour.

Cool and serve with sugar and cream. ANON.

51 QUICK PUFF PUDDING.

Sift with one pint flour one teaspoonful baking powder and a little salt. Stir in milk until a soft batter is produced. Put as many well greased cups as you desire in a steamer, and into each cup put a tablespoonful of the batter, then a layer of strawberries or any other fruit you may desire. Cover with another spoonful of batter and steam twenty minutes. Very nice.

Serve with sweet sauce. ANON.

52 SUET PUDDING.

2 cups flour.

2 teaspoonfuls baking powder.

1 cup chopped seedless raisins

1 cup chopped suet.

½ teaspoonful cinnamon.

½ cup white sugar.

1 teaspoonful salt.

Mix all together with the flour and moisten with sweet

milk to a very stiff batter   Grease dish and steam two and
one-half or three hours.

SAUCE

1 cup sugar with two teaspoonfuls flour.

½ cup butter.

1 cup boiling water.   Flavor with vanilla and nutmeg.

Boil until thick.   MRS. R. O. THOMEN.

53   STEAMED PUDDING.

1 egg.

1 cup molasses.

½ cup sweet milk.

1 tablespoonful butter.

½ teaspoonful soda.

Pinch of salt—spices to taste.

½ cup raisins.

Flour to make a batter the consistency of cake. Steam
one and one-half hours. Serve with sweet sauce.

                    MRS. MARY IRWIN, Danville, Iowa.

54   SNOW PUDDING.

1 ounce gelatine dissolved in one pint of boiling water.
Let stand until cool and add juice of one large or two small
lemons. One-half pound sugar. Whites of two eggs. Mix
all with gelatine and beat until it thickens. Put in a mould.
Serve with custard.   MRS. S. W. PIERCE.

55   COTTAGE PUDDING.

1 egg.

1 cup sugar.

1 cup sweet milk.

1 pint flour.

3 teaspoonfuls baking powder. Bake.

                    MRS. J. C. SCOTT.

56   QUEEN OF PUDDINGS.

1 pint fine bread crumbs.
1 quart milk.
1 cup sugar.
Yelks of four eggs.
Grated rind of one lemon.
Butter size of an egg. Bake. Layer of jelly.
After baking; then whites of eggs.
    1 cup powdered sugar.   MRS. J. W. BARNEY.

57   FOAM PUDDING.

Bake apples. Dig out all inside for use. To one-half dozen apples use whites of two eggs. Sweeten to taste. Juice of one lemon. Before serving beat together. Serve with cream.   MRS. J. W. BARNEY.

58   STEAMED PUDDING.

2 cups sour milk.
½ cup molasses.
2 cups flour.
2 cups corn meal.
1 teaspoonful soda. Salt. Steam one and one half hours. Add fruit if you like.   MRS J. C. SCOTT.

59   STEAMED SUET PUDDING.

1 cup chopped suet.
1 cup raisins or currants.
1 cup sweet milk.
1 cup molasses.
½ cup sugar.
2 cups flour.
1 teaspoonful salt.
2 teaspoonfuls baking powder.
2 eggs.

Season with spices. Put in a buttered basin and steam two hours.

SAUCE.

1 cup sugar.

2 tablespoonfuls butter.

1½ tablespoonfuls flour.

2 cups boiling water.

Yelks of two eggs. Whites beaten and put in last. This should be as light as a feather.   MRS. R M. CRAIL.

60   ORANGE PUDDING.

8 oranges cut up fine.

1 quart sweet milk.

2 tablespoonfuls corn starch.

6 tablespoonfuls sugar.

Pinch of salt. Yelks of six eggs. Make the custard and stir in the oranges after you take it off the stove. Make an icing of the whites of the eggs. One cup of sugar. Beat until thick—a long time. Dish up custard and put some of the icing on each dish.   ANON.

61   KENTUCKY PUDDING.

3 eggs.

1 cup sugar.

½ cup butter.

½ cup flour.   •

1 teacup jam or small fruit.

1 teaspoonful soda dissolved in three teaspoonfuls of butter milk. Cinnamon and nutmeg to taste Mix well together and bake slowly in a pudding pan. Serve with sauce.   MRS JAMES KETNER.

62 PRUNE PUDDING.

Whites of ten eggs beaten very stiff. ·

1 cup cooked prunes sifted through a colander, stirred very lightly into the eggs. Bake slowly just a few minutes Handle carefully, as it falls easily. MRS. R. M. CRAIL.

63 ENGLISH PLUM PUDDING.

1 cup sour milk

1 cup suet chopped fine.

1 cup molasses.

1 cup sugar.

1 cup raisins.

1 cup currants.

1 cup grated bread crumbs

2 cups flour.

1 teaspoonful salt.

½ teaspoonful each cloves, cinnamon and allspice.

1 even tablespoonful soda. Steam about four hours.

MRS. A. C. PIERCE.

64 BAKED BANANAS.

Put into a bowl—

3 tablespoonfuls butter.

6 tablespoonfuls sugar.

3 tablespoonfuls lemon juice.

Set the bowl into a pan of hot water so as to melt the butter. Peel the bananas and lay them in a shallow baking pan It must be perfectly clean and the bananas must not touch each other Baste the fruit with the mixture in the bowl, and bake for half an hour, basting three times more. Nice for an entree or dessert. ANON.

VI.

COOKIES.

47

65   GINGER COOKIES

1 cup sugar.

1 cup New Orleans molasses.

¾ cup shortening.

2 eggs.

2 teaspoonfuls soda dissolved in one third cup boiling water. Tablespoonful ginger Flour to make a rather soft dough. Roll thin and bake in a quick oven.

MRS. J. C. SCOTT.

66   SPICE COOKIES.

2 cups dark molasses

1 cup sugar.

1 cup lard.

1 cup buttermilk.

3 eggs—(save whites of two for icing).

1 teaspoonful ginger, allspice, nutmeg, cinnamon, lemon and vanilla.

½ pound raisins chopped.

A few currants and minced citron.

1 tablespoonful soda. Put fruit and spices in flour.

MRS. H. G. HIGINBOTHAM.

67   SUGAR BISCUIT.

1 quart flour.

1 cup sugar.

3 teaspoonfuls baking powder.

2 tablespoonfuls lard.

2 eggs.

¾ pint milk.

Sift together flour, salt, sugar and baking powder. Rub in lard—(cold). Add beaten eggs and milk. Mix smooth and drop with a spoon. Sift sugar over the top.

MRS. S. Q. BROWN.

68 CREAM DOUGHNUTS.

½ cup sour cream. Fill the cup with butter milk.

1 cup granulated sugar

2 eggs

Beat all together and add a level teaspoonful soda, a little salt, and flour enough to roll. Fry in hot lard.

DAISY McCLURE

69 DOUGHNUTS

1 cup sweet milk.

1 cup sugar.

½ cup butter.

3 cups flour.

2 eggs.

2 teaspoonfuls baking powder

Ground cinnamon or other spice to taste.

MRS W. W. BASKIN.

70 SOFT GINGER COOKIES

1 cup butter.

1 cup New Orleans molasses.

1 cup C sugar.

½ teaspoonful powdered alum dissolved in a little hot water.

1 cup cold water.

1 teaspoonful ginger. Stir all well, and last add two teaspoonfuls of soda dissolved in warm water. Mix in flour—soft. Handle with pancake turner or drop from a spoon. MRS. JOSEPHINE BLAKELY.

71 HERMITS.

1½ cups white sugar.

1 cup soft butter.

½ cup molasses.

3 eggs.

· ½ teaspoonful soda dissolved in one-half cup sour milk.

Cinnamon and spices and nutmeg. Flour to thicken and roll like cookies. Add one cup chopped raisins if liked. Bake in quick oven. MRS. JOSEPHINE BLAKELY.

VII.

CAKES.

72 CHOCOLATE CAKE.

1 cup brown sugar.

½ cup butter.

½ cup sweet milk.

2 cups flour.

Yelks of three eggs.

1 teaspoonful soda

DARK PART.

1 cup brown sugar.

1 cup grated chocolate.

½ cup sweet milk.

½ teaspoonful vanilla. Boil and let cool and mix with first part. Bake in square tin. Ice if preferred.

Mrs. W. W. Cook.

73 SILVER CAKE.

2 cups sugar—half pulverized).

2½ cups sifted flour.

½ cup butter.

¾ cup sweet milk.

½ tablespoonful soda

Whites of eight eggs.

1 teaspoonful cream tartar. Stir the butter and sugar to a cream. Add the eggs well beaten, then flour ; lastly the milk and soda. Mrs. W. W. Baskin.

74 WHITE CITRON CAKE.

1 pound sugar—(sifted).

1 pound flour.

1 pound butter.

½ pound almonds.

½ pound candied lemon.

¼ pound citron.

8 eggs. After the butter is beaten to a cream add the beaten eggs and then the flour. Beat for an hour and add other ingredients. Mrs. W. W. Baskin.

75   SNOW CAKE.

Whites of ten eggs beaten to a stiff froth. Sift lightly
on this one and one-half cups of fine white or pulverized
sugar. Stir well and add one cup flour mixed with one
teaspoonful cream tartar. Flavor with lemon or vanilla.

Mrs Annie Thurston.

76   CONFECTIONER'S CAKE.

1 large cup sugar—(half pulverized).
½ cup butter.
½ cup milk
2 cups flour
3 eggs
2 teaspoonfuls baking powder. Take out half the
batter and add to it one-half cup stoned raisins, cinnamon,
cloves and nutmeg. Bake in jelly tins and place in alternate layers, light and dark, with frosting between.

Mrs. W W. Baskin.

77   FAVORITE SNOW CAKE.

Beat one cup butter to a cream. Add one and one-
half cups flour. Stir thoroughly together. Add one cup
corn starch, one cup sweet milk in which three teaspoonfuls
baking powder have been dissolved Lastly add the whites
of eight eggs and two cups sugar well beaten together.
Flavor Bake in layers and put together with icing.

Mrs. Annie Thurston

78   ORANGE CAKE.

2 coffee cups sugar —(one granulated—one pulverized).
2 coffee cups flour.
½ coffee cup cold water.
Whites of four eggs – yelks of five eggs.
2 teaspoonfuls baking powder. Beat yelks and sugar

together. Add flour and baking powder and water, and lastly the beaten whites. Then take the juice and grated rind of one large orange and stir in the batter. Bake in layers. Make frosting of whites of two eggs; six table-spoonfuls sugar; juice and grated rind of one-half orange. Spread on layers.   MRS. W. W. BASKIN.

79   SPICED LAYER CAKE.

1 cup brown sugar.

1 cup molasses

1 cup cold coffee.

1 whole egg and two yelks

1 tablespoonful soda.

½ teaspoonful all kinds spices.

1 cup shortening. Use drippings, or lard even, is pre-ferable to butter. Flour to make a rather stiff batter. Bake in layers. Put together with icing.

                         MRS. M. A. WINANS.

80   JAM CAKE.

1 cup sugar.

¾ cup butter.

2 cups flour.

3 eggs

¾ cup blackberry jam.

1 teaspoonful soda dissolved in three tablespoonfuls sour cream or buttermilk.

1 nutmeg.

1 teaspoonful allspice.

1 teaspoonful vanilla.

1 teaspoonful lemon.

½ teaspoonful cloves.

1 tablespoonful cinnamon   Bake in layers. Put to-gether with boiled white icing or white caramel.

                    MRS. H. G. HIGINBOTHAM.

81 FIG CAKE.

Use for cake part, recipe for ocean foam. Bake in two square layers. Take one pound figs—cut up and steam until soft. Chop fine. Seed one pound of raisins, chop fine also. Add one cup sugar, one-half cup butter and hot water enough to moisten. Put this between the layers of cake. Very nice. MRS. A. L. BARNES.

82 MARBLE CAKE.

1 cup sugar.

½ cup butter. Rub these to a cream and divide into two parts, and use one for the light and one for the dark part of the cake.

DARK PART.

1 cup molasses.

½ cup milk.

1 cup flour

2 eggs—(yelks)

1 teaspoonful baking powder.

½ teaspoonful cloves.

½ teaspoonful cinnamon.

1 teaspoonful allspice.

LIGHT PART.

2 eggs—(whites).

1 teaspoonful baking powder.

½ cup milk.

1 cup flour. MRS. L. S. SARGENT.

83 BLACK FRUIT CAKE

1 pound sugar.

1 pound butter.

1 pound citron.

1 pound currants

2 pounds raisins.

1½ pounds flour.

¾ cup brandy.

12 eggs

1 teaspoonful soda

1 teaspoonful salt.

1 cup molasses. Divide the flour into two equal parts. Into one part put the following spices.

1 teaspoonful cinnamon.

1 nutmeg—(grated).

¼ teaspoonful cloves.

⅔ teaspoonful allspice. Mix the fruit thoroughly with the remaining half of the flour. Cream the butter and sugar Add the yelks of eggs. Dissolve the soda in a little warm water Stir it into the molasses and pour into the cake bowl Add the flour and spices. Stir smooth, then put in the flour and fruit. Add the stiffly beaten whites of eggs. Stir the batter until thoroughly mixed, then pour into baking tins lined with buttered paper. This will make two very large loaves. Bake in a moderate oven for two hours. Mrs. L. S. Sargent.

84 NUT CAKE.

2 eggs

1 cup sugar

½ cup butter – (not generous).

½ cup milk

1½ cups flour.

1 teaspoonful baking powder.

1 large cup nuts, chopped fine, and well flavored.

Flavor with vanilla. Helen G. McClure.

85 CHOCOLATE CAKE.

½ cup butter.

1½ cups sugar

Yelks four eggs

½ cup milk.

2 scant cups flour

2 spoonfuls baking powder.

Add three ounces Baker's chocolate dissolved in one-half cup boiling water. Lastly, whites of eggs. Vanilla. Icing for same.

1 ounce Baker's chocolate.

1 cup sugar. *

½ cup milk. Boil till thick. Remove from fire and beat till cool enough to use.   DAISY McCLURE.

86   SPICE CAKE.

1 tumbler molasses.

1 tumbler sugar.

1 tumbler butter.

1 tumbler sweet milk.

3 tumblers flour.

3 eggs.

1 teaspoonful soda.

2 teaspoonfuls each kind of spice. HELEN G. McCLURE.

87   MARSH MALLOW CAKE.

CAKE PART.

½ cup milk or water.

1½ cups sugar.

½ cup butter.

1½ cups flour.

½ cup corn starch.

1 teaspoonful baking powder.

Whites of six eggs.

FILLING.

2 large tablespoonfuls gelatine dissolved in seven table-spoonfuls hot water. Add gradually one pound confectioners sugar. Beat one-half hour. Put into a pan to mould, size of cake.   MISS HESLEP.

88 CORN STARCH CAKE.

12 eggs—(whites).
3 cups sugar.
3 cups flour.
1 cup butter.
1 cup corn starch.—Vanilla.
1 cup milk.
3 teaspoonfuls baking powder. MRS. J. C. SCOTT.

89 OCEAN FOAM CAKE.

2 cups sugar.
½ cup butter.
1 cup water.
3 cups flour.
3 teaspoonfuls baking powder.
Whites of eight eggs beaten to a stiff froth and added last. Flavor. MRS. J. C. SCOTT.

90 PRINCE ALBERT CAKE.

WHITE PART.

1 cup powdered sugar.
Small one half cup butter.
½ cup milk.
2 cups flour.
1 teaspoonful baking powder.
Whites of four eggs.

DARK PART.

1 cup brown sugar.
½ cup milk.
2 cups flour.
Small one-half cup butter.
1 teaspoonful baking powder.
Yelks of four eggs.
1 teaspoonful cinnamon.
½ teaspoonful cloves. Nutmeg.

1 cup fruit —(raisins, currants and citron).   Bake in layers with icing on dark layer and jelly on white layer.

MRS L. S SARGENT.

91   MOLASSES CAKE.

1 egg.
½ cup sugar.
½ cup molasses.
1½ cups flour.
½ cup sour milk.
2 tablespoonfuls butter.
1 teaspoonful soda.
Cinnamon and ginger.   Very nice with whipped cream, flavored with nutmeg.   MRS. J. C SCOTT.

92   CREAM CAKE.

Break two eggs in a cup and fill up the cup with thick sweet cream.   Add —
1 cup sugar.
1 cup flour.
1 teaspoonful cream tartar.
½ teaspoonful soda.   Put all together and stir as little as possible.   The less the better.   MRS W. W. BASKIN.

93   MOCK LADY CAKE

3 cups flour.
2 cups sugar.
½ cup butter.
1 cup sweet milk.
4 eggs —(whites).
1 teaspoonful cream tartar.
½ teaspoonful soda.   Beat the butter and sugar to a cream.   Add the whites of eggs and beat thoroughly.   Next the flour and cream tartar.   Milk and soda last.   Flavor.
MRS W. W. BASKIN.

94   CHOCOLATE HONGAT.

1½ cups sugar. } Creamed together.
½ cup butter. }

1½ cups flour.
½ cup sweet milk.
3 eggs, beaten well.
½ pound Baker's chocolate, grated.
2 teaspoonfuls baking powder in flour. Add five table-spoonfuls sugar to the grated chocolate and three of boiling water and stir over the fire until smooth Add this to the butter and sugar, then add the eggs, then the flour and milk alternately. Mix thoroughly and bake in three or four layers. Put together with icing flavored with vanilla.

KATE L. SCOTT.

95   BEEFSTEAK CAKE.

¾ cup butter.
2 cups sugar.
2 cups flour.
3 eggs – (whites).
1 cup sweet milk.
3 teaspoonfuls baking powder.
Bake two thirds of the mixture on two round tins and to the remainder add three yelks.

96   HARRISON CAKE.

1 cup shortening.
¾ cup butter.
⅓ cup lard.
2 cups sugar.
¾ cup molasses.
1½ cups water.
4 cups flour.
3 eggs.
1 teaspoonful soda.
1 nutmeg.
1 tablespoonful cloves.
1 tablespoonful cinnamon.
½ pound citron.
1 pound currants.
2 pounds raisins Bake in a very slow oven three hours. Or if in two loaves, one and one-half hours.

MRS. BERT TYLER.

3 tablespoonfuls molasses.

1 cup raisins.

½ cup flour and all kinds of spices. Bake in one cake and place between the other two with jelly between.

MRS. G. F. SANTELLE.

96 FRUIT CAKE.

½ pound butter.

½ pound flour.

½ pound sugar.

1 pound raisins.

1 pound currants.

½ pound citron.

6 eggs.

1 tablespoonful cinnamon.

½ tablespoonful cloves.

1½ nutmegs.

1 wine glass wine.

1 wine glass brandy.

1 wine glass rose water. Wine can be used instead of rose water. Line the tin with buttered paper and bake slowly two hours. It will not raise any.

MRS. R. M. CRAIL.

97 ANGELS FOOD.

Whites of eleven eggs.

1½ tumblers sifted granulated sugar.

1 tumbler sifted flour.

1 teaspoonful vanilla.

1 teaspoonful cream tartar. Sift flour and cream tartar together several times. Beat eggs to a stiff froth on a plat-ter. Add the sugar lightly, then the flour gently. Lastly the vanilla. Do not stop until you put it in a pan. Bake in a moderate oven forty-five minutes. MRS. TROVINGER.

99 SPANISH BUNS.

1½ cups brown sugar.
½ cup butter.
½ cup milk.
2 cups flour.
3 eggs.
2 teaspoonfuls baking powder.
Spices to taste.
Bake in patty pans and ice. MRS. BABBAGE.

100 GINGER CAKE.

2 eggs.
1 cup sour milk.
1½ cups brown sugar.
½ cup butter.
½ cup molasses.
2 cups flour.
1 teaspoonful soda. EMMA STEADMAN.

101 MAUD S. CAKE.

THE CUSTARD.

½ cup milk.
8 tablespoonfuls grated chocolate.
5 tablespoonfuls granulated sugar.
Let boil until it thickens a little.
1½ cups light brown sugar.
⅔ cup butter.
3 eggs.
½ cup milk.
½ cup flour. Then stir in the custard, after which add
two cups more of flour and two teaspoonfuls baking powder.
Bake in layers about one inch thick and ice with following:
1 cup sugar.
½ cup milk. Let boil eight minutes and season with a
small piece of butter and vanilla. Cut in squares. Do not
put the layers together. MRS. R. M. CRAIL.

102 CARAMEL FILLING.

2 cups brown sugar.

1 cup cream or milk.

2 tablespoonfuls butter.

1 teaspoonful vanilla. Boil till ropy. Chopped walnut meats put in, make it very nice. Mrs. J. C. Scott.

103 ICE CREAM FROSTING.

2 cups sugar.

3 eggs. Whites beaten to a stiff froth. Boil and pour sugar over the eggs, beating all together rapidly.

Mrs. H. G. Higinbotham.

104 ICING.

Take white of egg and stir in pulverized sugar until of the right consistency to spread. Flavor. Icing made in this way will never break. Mrs. J. C. Scott.

105 BOILED ICING.

1 cup granulated sugar.

⅓ cup boiling water.

⅓ teaspoonful cream tartar. Boil six minutes. Beat white of one egg to stiff froth. Gradually beat into it the boiled sugar pouring it in a thin stream. Beat five minutes after the last of the sugar has been added. Flavor. Do not stir the sugar while it is being boiled Anon.

106 HOW TO STONE RAISINS.

Free them from the stems. Cover with boiling water and let them stand a few minutes and the seed can be easily removed. Mrs. J. C. Scott.

VIII.

PICKLES.

[67]

107 CHOW CHOW.

¼ peck onions.

¼ peck green tomatoes.

1½ heads cauliflower.

5 heads celery.

1½ dozen small cucumbers.

3 large green peppers.

3 large red peppers. Cut all in small pieces and let stand over night in salt—'about one pint). Drain dry and cook tender (thirty minutes) in two quarts vinegar. Skim out and add to the vinegar :

1 ounce white mustard seed.

½ ounce black mustard seed. .

2 ounces yellow ground mustard.

½ ounce turmeric powder.

¼ cup flour.

1 horse radish root, grated.

½ pint water.

¼ pint salt.

2 large cups sugar. Mix the ground stuff with the water. Pour in boiling vinegar. Add seed.

Mrs. B. J. Dawson.

108 FRENCH PICKLES.

2½ quarts sliced green tomatoes.

2½ quarts sliced cucumbers.

1 quart sliced onions.

2 handsfull salt. Let stand twenty-four hours, then drain and add :

½ ounce celery seed.

½ ounce allspice.

1 teacup white mustard seed —whole.

1 teaspoonful black pepper.

1 tablespoonful turmeric.

1 pound brown sugar.

3 quarts good vinegar. Heat vinegar, sugar and tur-

meric scalding hot and pour over the pickles.

Mrs. W. W. Baskin.

109   MANGOES.

3 ounces stick cinnamon.

½ ounce whole cloves.

½ ounce whole allspice.

½ ounce whole peppercorn.

A little mace.   Roll these spices.

½ ounce race ginger, boiled and sliced.

1 pound white mustard seed.

3 bulbs garlic, separated and peeled.

1 pound horse radish, cut like dice.

1 ounce turmeric mixed smoothly with a little vinegar.

4 pounds brown sugar dissolved in vinegar, which is one part wine and two parts vinegar—one and one-half gallons in all. Soak mangoes in strong salt water, strong enough to float an egg, without opening melons, for nearly a week. After soaking, remove seeds and boil in vinegar until tender enough to pierce with a straw.   Mrs. Hale.

110   PICCALILLY.

5 quarts cabbage chopped fine.

2 quarts tomatoes—green.

1 quart onions

½ pint green peppers.

2½ quarts vinegar.

½ ounce turmeric.

½ ounce celery seed

1 tablespoonful ginger.

2 pounds sugar.   Salt to taste   Put all together and let boil one hour.   Seal while hot.   Mrs W. W. Baskin.

111   SPICED CURRANTS OR CHERRIES

3 pounds white sugar.

5 pounds ripe currants.

1 tablespoonful each cinnamon, cloves, allspice, nutmeg. Boil currants one hour, then add sugar, spices and one-half pint vinegar. Boil one half hour longer. If cherries are used pit and chop quite fine. Nice with meat.

Mrs. J. C. Scott.

112 BOURDER SAUCE.

1 peck green tomatoes.
4 small head cabbage.
1 dozen onions.
5 green peppers.
½ pound white mustard seed.
1 gallon vinegar.
3½ pounds brown sugar.
2 gills salt.
¼ pound allspice.
½ pound celery seed.
1 ounce turmeric. Mix cold. Put in a stone jar and tie up with a cloth and plate. Mrs. Babbage.

113 TOMATO CATSUP.

1 peck ripe tomatoes Cook and strain through a sieve. Add to the juice four common sized onions, chopped fine. Let it boil down Steep in one quart of vinegar.

3 red peppers
2 tablespoonfuls mustard.
2 tablespoonfuls allspice.
2 tablespoonfuls cinnamon. Strain it into the juice. Add
1 pound brown sugar.
½ tea cup salt. Let it cook down thick enough for use. Seal in bottles while hot. The onions may be omitted if preferred Mrs. L. S. Sargent.

IX.

CONFECTIONERY.

114   BUTTER SCOTCH.

3 tablespoonfuls molasses.
2 tablespoonfuls sugar.
2 tablespoonfuls water.
1 tablespoonful butter.
Pinch of soda before taking up.   RHEA BABBAGE.

115   CANDY CREAM OR FONDANT.

First with glucose—
2 cups granulated sugar.
1 heaping tablespoonful glucose.
1 cup boiling water—stir well.
Second with cream tartar.
3 cups granulated sugar.
1 cup water.
⅛ teaspoonful cream tartar. Do not stir. Boil either
of the above rapidly until it will form a soft ball between
the thumb and finger, when tested in water. Remove from
the fire and when luke warm, stir until it becomes white
and dry. Then put on a moulding board and knead as you
would bread, until it becomes creamy. It may be kept in
this condition for several days, by covering with a damp
cloth.   ANON.

116   BON BONS

Take of the above cream any amount and place in a
bowl. Set in water over a slow fire. When melted, dip in
sections of oranges or whole kernels of nuts, dates, or figs,
etc., and when cooled you will have a dainty morsel. The
Brazilian nuts being especially fine.   MRS. R. O. THOMEV.

117   NUT CREAMS.

The above prepared cream mixed with any kind of
good nuts, dates, cocoanut, figs etc., whole or chopped, and
formed into fanciful shapes, makes delicious candies.
          ANON.

118   CHOCOLATE DROPS.

Form the above cream into desired shapes and place on paraffine or buttered paper to harden. When cold, dip into chocolate which has been melted with a little butter and a small piece of paraffine and a few drops of vanilla.

ANON.

119   SUGARED WALNUTS.

2½ cups sugar—brown
½ pint water.
Small lump butter
1 teaspoonful vanilla   Boil until it hardens in water. Remove from fire and put in walnut meats. Stir until meats are sugary.   KATE L. SCOTT.

120   CREAM CANDY.

3 teacups of sugar (or two pounds) to one pint of boiling water. Butter size of walnut to each pound, and one teaspoonful vanilla Try in cold water. Take off when it snaps. Pour on marble slab.   MRS. KATE O REILLY.

121   MOLASSES CANDY.

2 cups molasses.
1 cup sugar.
1 tablespoonful vinegar.   Butter size of a hickory nut. Boil briskly twenty minutes, stirring all the time.

MRS. STEVENSON.

122   COCOANUT MACAROONS.

White of one egg.
1 fresh grated cocoanut or one half package.
½ pound confectioners sugar.   Work into a stiff paste and form with the hands into small cakes. Lay on butter paper. Dust with powdered sugar. Put in a hot oven to brown.   MRS. JOSEPHINE BLAKELY.

123   ORANGE ICE.

6 oranges—grated—peel and juice.
2 pounds sugar.
1 gallon water.   ANON.

124   PINE-APPLE ICE.

1 can pine apples cut fine.
1½ pounds sugar.
1 gallon water. When partly frozen add whites of four
eggs. Stir fast.   ANON.

125   LEMON ICE.

6 lemons.
2 pounds sugar.
1 gallon water. Whites of four eggs.   ANON.

126   BANANA ICE.

Same as lemon, using two bananas.
                                          MRS. R. M. CRAIL.

127   ICE CREAM.

3 quarts milk.
1 quart cream.
7 small tablespoonfuls flour.
20 tablespoonfuls sugar. Flavor to taste. Heat milk
in a double kettle. Add flour previously mixed smooth,
with a little of the milk. Cook until it loses the taste of
the flour, stirring constantly. Let cool and strain through
a wire sieve. Add sugar, cream and flavoring. Freeze.
                                          MRS. ELLIS POLAND.

128   WHIPPED CREAM.

To a coffee cup of cream add the whites of two eggs,
two tablespoonfuls of sugar and a little flavoring extract.
Beat all together. A regular egg beater will do the work
most rapidly.
This quantity will make a quart—after it is beaten so
as to stand alone, when dropped from off a spoon.
The cream should be rather thick and perfectly sweet.
The cooler the cream the quicker it becomes thick.
                                          HOME RECORD.

X.

MISCELLA-
NEOUS.

129   NEAPOLITAINOES.

Make enough puff paste for a pie. Roll into a sheet half an inch thick and cut into strips three inches by one-one half, bake in a quick oven. When cold spread with jam or jelly half the strips. Stick the others over in pairs. Cover with icing.   ANON.

130   HAMBURG CREAM.

Stir together grated rind and juice of two large lemons and one cup sugar. Add the well beaten yelks of eight eggs. Put in double boiler, and stir for three minutes. Remove from fire. Add the well beaten whites of the eggs and serve when cold in custard cups.

MRS. G. F. SAWTELLE.

131   NESSELRODE PUDDING

1 quart cream.

6 eggs— whites . A little of the cream, say one-half pint or so scalded, with the eggs beaten thoroughly with beater.

½ of a pine-apple grated and sweetened.

½ pound of candied cherries chopped fine, mixed with pine apple. Sweeten and freeze.   MRS. L. S SARGENT.

132   NEAPOLITAN CREAM.

NO. 1.

1 quart cream whipped to a stiff froth.

1 tablespoonful gelatine dissolved in one half cup hot water. Let cool and strain into cream.

1 cup pulverized sugar.

1 teaspoonful vanilla. Pack in a freezer and let it remain several hours. Delicious. MRS H. G. HIGINBOTHAM.

133   NEAPOLITAN CREAM.

NO 2.

½ pound crystalized fruit, minced and covered with the juice of one orange. Let stand three or four hours. Stir lightly into the quart of whipped cream, from bottom to top.

1 teaspoonful vanilla. Pack same as number one.

MRS. H. G. HIGINBOTHAM

134 CREAM PUFFS.

1 pint water.

½ pound butter. Boil water and butter for a few minutes, then stir in three-fourths pound of flour. Let it thicken to a paste. Put it to cool on a platter. Beat up ten eggs Mix together one half teaspoonful of dry soda with eggs and paste. Drop with a teaspoon on buttered pans. Bake from twenty to twenty five minutes in quick oven. Pan not to be stirred. Cream, one quart—milk, boiled. Four eggs two cups sugar, one cup flour. Mix together, then stir in the milk while boiling When cool, flavor with lemon. Mrs. Mary R. Seymour.

135 SCALLOPED CORN.

Fix the same as scalloped oysters, using corn instead.
Mrs. R. M. Crail.

136 TUTTI FRUTTI.

Into a wide top bottle or jar that can be closed tightly, put one pint of best alcohol and add one pound sugar. Shake thoroughly, then put in about equal quantities of strawberries, raspberries, cherries, (stoned) peaches (cut in small pieces) also pine apple (shredded). Other varieties of fruit may be added. This operation may be commenced early in the season, and in order to preserve the proportions, one may put in a one half pound each of the different fruits, and in this way it will be easier to keep track of the proportions which must not vary. Add one half pound of sugar and one half pound of fruit at the same time.

More alcohol will not be needed unless a large amount of fruit is added —say five pounds - after which another pint may be put in, or one quart, if there are signs of fermentation Care should be taken in opening the jar to add fruits as they ripen, that the cover is replaced as soon as possible.

Keep the jar in a cool place and in the dark. This preserve is excellent with cold meats or poultry, or used in the same way as cranberry sauce. Mrs. W W. Baskin.

137 FRUIT SALAD.

1½ pounds lump sugar.

1 quart warm water. Box of Cox's gelatine. Juice and rind of four lemons. Dissolve and strain. When it commences to jelly, put in fruit. Slice one-half dozen oranges, one-half dozen bananas, one can grated pine-apple.

MRS. BABBAGE.

138 SALAD CREAM.

4 tablespoonfuls butter.
1 tablespoonful flour.
1 tablespoonful sugar.
1 teaspoonful salt.
1 teaspoonful dry mustard. ̄
½ cup vinegar.
1 cup milk.

3 eggs and a speck of cayenne pepper. Let the butter get hot. Add flour and stir until smooth, being careful not to brown. Add milk, stir and boil up. Place the sauce pan in another of hot water. Beat eggs, salt and mustard. Add vinegar and stir into the boiling mixture. Stir until it thickens. MRS. J. C. SCOTT.

139 LETTUCE SALAD. •

2 hard boiled eggs and two potatoes chopped fine.

1 bunch lettuce chopped separately, after which mix together with a dressing of vinegar, salt, pepper, sugar and a little onion and celery. Garnish with lettuce leaves and sliced cold boiled eggs. MRS. BABBAGE.

140 LETTUCE AND TOMATO SALAD.

Choose bright, firm, medium sized tomatoes. Peel them and place on ice. Select the white inner part of lettuce. Have in readiness a mayonaise dressing, or make a cream dressing. (The cream may be sweet or sour, but must be rich), as follows:

Beat one-half pint of cream to a thick mass. To the hard boiled yelks of three eggs add one raw yelk and mix together until they form a thick paste. . Season with one teaspoonful salt, one teaspoonful sugar, one teaspoonful mustard—(if liked), two tablespoonfuls vinegar. When all these have been thoroughly blended, stir the mixture a little at a time into the whipped cream. Arrange the lettuce in groups of two or three leaves each to form a cup, placing each group on a separate plate or clustering all together on a large platter, and into each cup formed by the leaves, put a heaping teaspoonful of dressing.

Cut the tomatoes in half and place the flat side of each half into each spoonful of dressing, so that the lettuce leaves curl up over the edges of the tomato.

Mrs. L. S. Sargent.

141 BEET SALAD.

Cut cold boiled beets into cubes, and moisten them with any kind of salad dressing. This is a handsome and palatable dish.

Beets and potatoes used together in the same way, make a nice salad also. Mrs. J. C. Scott.

142 TOMATO SALAD.

Rub through a coarse sieve one can of tomatoes. Cover with cold water a half box of Cox's gelatine and let it stand for a half hour or more. Then pour in enough hot water to thoroughly dissolve it. Then mix with one full pint of the strained tomatoes Add a little salt. Mould. Serve on lettuce leaves with mayonaise dressing. If desired, put in dice of celery. Mrs. Josephine Blakely.

143 CHEESE STRAWS.

1 cup grated cheese.
1 cup flour. Pinch cayenne pepper. Salt—spoon salt.
½ cup butter rubbed in as for pastry. Roll thin, cut in narrow strips and bake in quick oven. Daisy McClure.

144 TOMATO JELLY.

1 quart can tomatoes.
½ box gelatine dissolved in one-half cup water. Strain tomatoes and cook for about twenty minutes. Season to taste Add the gelatine and pour into mould after wetting mould with cold water. Helen G. McClure.

145 CHEESE FONDU.

1 cup rolled crackers or bread crumbs.
1 cup milk.

¾ cup grated cheese.

2 eggs, whites and yelks beaten separately very light. Add all together and bake twenty minutes in a very quick oven. Serve immediately.   MRS. J. C. SCOTT.

146   SALTED PEA-NUTS.

Take raw pea-nuts and after removing shells, pour boiling water over them. After standing a few minutes slip the outside brown skin off.

Place in a dripping pan and partly brown. Then put in a little butter and salt and let them get quite brown.

ANON.

147   FRUIT PIN WHEELS.

Mix together and rub through a sieve—
1 pint flour.
1 tablespoonful sugar.
½ teaspoonful salt.
2 teaspoonfuls baking powder. Into this mixture rub two generous tablespoonfuls of butter. Wet with a scant one half pint of milk. Sprinkle the board with flour, and putting the dough upon it, roll down to a large square, about one-half inch thick. Spread on this one large tablespoonful butter, one cup sugar and one cup currants. Grate a little nutmeg over all and roll up like a jelly roll. Cut in slices about three fourths of an inch thick and lay in buttered pan. Do not let the slices touch each other. Bake in quick oven for about twelve minutes. Nice for luncheon or tea.   ANON.

148   SALTED ALMONDS.

Blanche a quantity of almonds and for each cupful add a tablespoonful melted butter or salad oil. Stir well and let them stand for an hour. Sprinkle with salt, allowing a tablespoonful for each cup. Put the almonds in a clean baking pan in a moderate oven and bake until a delicate brown; about one fourth of an hour. Place on the table at the beginning of the dinner and serve with crackers and cheese.   ANON.

149   TO BLANCHE ALMONDS.

Shell the nuts and pour boiling water over them. Let

them stand a minute and then throw into cold water. Rub
between the hands. ANON.

150 CORN OYSTERS.

Six ears of corn. Score and press out the grain. Separate two eggs. Beat the yelks. Add them to the corn.
Beat the whites and add them. Add a half teaspoonful salt,
a dash of pepper, two heaping tablespoonfuls flour. Mix
carefully. Two tablespoonfuls of fat in the frying pan.
When hot, drop in the mixture by tablespoonfuls. Brown
on one side, turn and brown on the other. L. C. BARNES.

151 RECIPE FOR CANNING CORN.

For every eight quarts of corn use one ounce of tar-
taric acid. Put corn in kettle. Cover with water Let
cook twenty minutes, then add the acid. Boil ten minutes
longer. Can in tin cans When you want to prepare for
the table, put a scant one half teaspoonful soda into a quart.
Add a little water. Let boil a few minutes, then drain dry.
Put in a little more water, butter, salt, pepper and cream if
you like. Serve hot. MRS MARY IRWIN, Danville, Iowa.

152 GRAPE JELLY.

Pick the grapes when they are half ripe. Wash carefully. Put to boil in small quantity of hot water. When
soft, pour into a bag to let drain. Take equal parts sugar
and juice and boil twenty minutes. Pour into glasses and
when cold lay discs of writing paper spread with white of
an egg. Cut to fit inside of glasses on top of jelly to
exclude the air. Tie cloth over top. EVELYN B. DAVIS.

153 MACARONI.

Break the macaroni into strongly salted boiling water.
Boil forty-five minutes. The secret of cooking macaroni is
to have the water boiling and keep it boiling until taken
from the fire. Then drain immediately and put into greased
baking dish a layer of macaroni, followed by a layer of
grated cheese alternate, until the dish is full, having a thick
layer of cheese on top. Place in a quick oven and let bake
twenty minutes or until brown. EVELYN B. DAVIS.

XI.
A HYGIENIC
DINNER.

A HYGIENIC DINNER.

Riding in Philadelphia one morning, I observed a sign over the front door of a large brick mansion.

The name was that of the greatest of Hygienic physicians, whom I had long wished to meet. I leaped from the car, rang the bell, audaciously determined to have a chat with the wonderful man, who could persuade thousands of people, both sick and well, to forego their accustomed table luxuries, for the sake of good bodily and mental health.

I hardly knew what gustatory enjoyments the disciples of that extremist might have; albeit I had spent several years at water cures and other sanitariums (not lunatic asylums); but I was determined to find out.

Asking for Dr. Trall I was conducted to a slender lady, not yet thirty, of very attractive appearance "I am Dr. Trall's daughter in-law,' she said; and this is a branch of his large cure. It followed that I received an urgent invitation to spend an entire day with the charming doctor, be initiated as to her system of water treatment and—eat a Hygienic dinner! You will have, therefore, in this article, directions for preparing certain kinds of food after the strictest so called Hygienic methods. Wide experience and much observation of invalids (there were a thousand at once in Clifton Sanitarium where I have spent much time) lead me to indorse these preparations heartily for dyspeptics. Even people supposed to be in health, by adopting a similar but less severe dietectic system, will be less subject to head aches, billious attacks, and that lassitude which is likely to be caused by impeded digestion and imperfect assimilation.

IMPRIMIS: Dr. Trall wholly discards animal food, not even allowing fish, eggs or milk (except for babes). Full-fed persons are often much benefitted by a temporary adoption of this plan; although there are undoubtedly many who crave or constitutionally demand flesh and kindred food.

SECUNDUS : Dr. Trall, perceiving that far too much use is made of salt, to the injury especially of the scrofulous and impure blooded, pulls the other way, and denies that the human system has any use for it.

TERTIUS : He objects to sugar made from sap and the juice of the cane, claiming that until nature has fully elaborated her saccharine material so that it has become organized and embodied in grains, fruits, etc., it is not worthy to build up the perfect man and woman. Moreover he insists that nature prepares nutrition IN DUE PROPORTION, and that when we add pure sugar (or impure rather), we are getting just so much more than the human system requires. In this last sense, he is probably nearly or quite correct.

Understanding what deprivations awaited me, I sat down to my Hygienic dinner (after the most hunger provoking bath I ever had) feeling that even I, nine tenths vegetarian by nature, would fail to be satisfied. At the tables were many business men of apparently large intelligence and good health, who of choice had for years followed the course of feeding prescribed by Dr. Trall.

One strict rule is to drink shortly before meals, but never during them, or within three hours thereafter. Some concession was made in the way of soup, of which here and there, one partook.

Green corn scraped, rather than cut from the cob was cooked in a little water. To this was added tomatoes which had been cooked and passed through a colander, the whole being boiled and rapidly stirred till thoroughly commingled. No salt! Although I should have pronounced such a mixture unhygienic, it no way interfered with my digestion, and was quite as palatable as our fashionable tomato-bisque which is prepared in the same way, substituting milk for corn, and adding salt.

Vegetables and legumes naturally took the place of meat, — roasted Irish potatoes, roasted and boiled yams, sliced beets (without vinegar) tenderly cooked cauliflower, turnips, boiled carrots, afterward nicely browned) and salad dressed with olive oil and flavored with sweet herbs; best of all, baked Hubbard squash! Not so much as a pinch of salt anywhere! But though I am fond of salt, I now perceived for the first time the true delicacy of vegetable food, and the peculiar self-flavor which makes each kind enjoy-

able unadulterated. There was all the difference between
smelling flowers separately or together. The keener sense
prefers the former.

These were cooked with elaborate care. The baked
potatoes and yams were squeezed open when taken from
the oven so that no condensing steam could make them
soggy. The boiled beans—at least the Lima and I think
the Navy also, were cooked in but one water, which was
allowed to almost wholly evaporate, so that they were served nearly dry with all their rich qualities conserved. They
were the best I ever ate.

Meantime the breadstuffs were mostly novel. No fermented bread was allowed, nor any prepared of white flour
alone, except by special prescription. First of all the true,
original Graham gems —so named because of precious value
as food! Trust no recipe but this for gems!

Perfect Graham flour, not too finely ground, and containing all the bran—that is the first requirement! Next, a
set of cast iron cup pans.—tin will not do; then a strong,
steady fire, much hotter than is required for bread. Put
your pans in to heat Then beat the flour rapidly and
lightly into cold water; (never pour the water on the flour)
until the dough is nearly as thick as ordinary pancake
dough. It must run, not drop, from the spoon. Fill the
cups nearly level—they must be hissing hot and will need
but the merest touch of butter), and bake twenty minutes
before opening the oven door. They will probably require
ten minutes longer to be thoroughly done. The hot iron
sears the bottom at once, the upper heat soon sears the top,
and fast as the water within is converted into steam, which
cannot escape, it separates their particles so that they turn
out very light. I have fed chiefly on Graham gems (more
or less perfect according to conditions) more than thirty
years—and still live! No other bread compares with them.

The Graham finger-rolls were however preferred at Dr.
Trall's table, and at one cure where I spent some time.
Pour boiling water on Graham flour, stirring until the
dough is of sufficient consistency to roll in the hands. Add
flour as you roll, and make them in size about as the name
indicates, baking them brown in a fairly hot oven.

Old-fashioned granular oatmeal was handed me, made
into bread prepared after an original method by Miss Julia
Coleman, professor of dietectics under Dr. Trall. I have

the recipe with others directly from Miss Coleman, who is a personal friend To one cup of oatmeal take three cups of cold water. Grease a hot cast iron spider lightly with butter, pour in the mixture, set on top of the stove, cover close and let it slowly bake twenty minutes; then uncover and bake till somewhat browned. This is incomparably better than the old Scotch oatmeal yeast cakes.

Dr. Trall's objection to fermented bread, amounts to this: The yeast germ feeds upon an essentially nutritive property of the grain, and wholly destroys it. The grain as the Lord made it is right; any chemical alteration or process of destruction makes it wrong.

If the reader ever chewed wheat, he has some idea of its delicate sweetness All grains, unrobbed and unadulterated, properly cooked, eaten without salt, are delicious, and form the most perfect food of man.

When, at our dinner, we were well through with the solids, I had so thoroughly enjoyed the meal that I could eat little more without a disagreeable sense of stuffing. Still I was there to learn, even at some cost. In addition they serve various mushes of oatmeal, graham, rye meal, barley meal (best of all), golden millet, buck-wheat meal, corn meal, with coarser preparations of Scotch groats (pronounced grouts), samp and hominy. Also German green corn—being whole grains of rye, cut while unripe, and almost equal to American green corn.

Miss Coleman's general rule for mushes is to use one part meal to four parts water, stirring it in slowly, never allowing the water to stop boiling; then set back where they will slowly bubble without burning for four hours. They are not to be stirred after once made You who prepare mush just before meal time, know nothing of its superlative excellence

We ate ours without cream, but some used fruit-juice, (any kind will do) slightly thickened to give it body. And to wind up, I—ate pie! two kinds!—pumpkin or squash for one, made to closely resemble the ordinary kind, by corn-starch thickening instead of milk or eggs. For additional sweetness, a syrup had been put in, made of the boiled down juice of pumpkins—and right good it made the pie! Sour apple pie is usually sweetened with jellied juice of sweet apples, or with figs, or dates. The kind I ate was made with figs, and exceedingly good. As to the crust, it was made of Graham flour and it was tender, being shortened with old fashioned granulated oatmeal. My mother, humoring my dyspepsia, used sometimes to sift a thin layer of cornmeal over a pie-tin, for pumpkin or custard pies, and if well baked, I ask no better crust.

To end our Hygienic dinner we were given fruits and nuts. Of all the food (which as you see was in unusual variety) nothing could have disturbed a delicate digestion, unless the diner had eaten both fruit and vegetables which together tend to create fermentation. With vegetables I do not class tomatoes, corn (unless very green), beans, peas or any leguminous food.

Above all things, eat your Hygienic food slowly and reverently, taking moderate mouthfuls and appreciating the delicate flavors brought out only by thorough mastication. And, when you have ended, thank God for a good dinner.

AMANDA T. JONES.

Addenda to "A Hygienic Dinner."

GRAHAM CARTWHEELS.

Pour thin Graham gem batter one quarter inch deep into round pie tins. Bake in a hot oven till brown. Put away till next morning. Then just before breakfast, lay them in the oven till crisp. Eat hot. The best bread I ever ate.

GRAHAM PIE.

Pour Graham gem batter one-half inch thick into pie-tins. Bake in a hot oven. Sp it and butter. Fill the lower part with nice fresh apple sauce or any good soft fruit. (Strawberries will answer on a pinch). Lay on the upper part, return to the oven till thoroughly hot. Eat with cream.

GEM PUDDING.

Cut or chop cold Graham gems into small pieces Put a layer of apples in a basin. Sprinkle on sugar and add seasoning of allspice, nutmeg or cinnamon if you like. Then put a layer of the gem pieces. Alternate apples and gems, seasoning as desired, till the basin is full. Add a cup of water. Cover and bake one hour. Then remove cover and brown. Eat warm or cold, with cream. White bread pudding is very nice, made in the same way.

GREEN CORN PUDDING.

One pint green corn scraped from the cobs. One quart of milk. Three eggs. Sweeten to taste. Bake three-quarters of an hour at least.

PEARL BARLEY DESSERT.

Cook a cupful of Pearl Barley thoroughly. Better soak over night, and cook some hours. Will require four cups water. When done and dry like rice, add the juice of six oranges and sugar to taste. Return to the oven and bake a full half hour. No dressing required.

GRAHAM RUSK.

Thoroughly dry pieces of Graham bread, or gems, in a slow oven, brown without burning. Pound up fine or break up and grind like coffee in a mill. Eat with milk. Cream makes it superlative.

QUEEN'S OAT CAKES.

Mix Scotch oatmeal (any kind will answer) with milk and cream (half and half)—one cup meal to three cups wetting. Let stand till swelled. Drop on buttered tins, spread out a half inch thick. Bake thoroughly. Eat hot or cold.

FINIS.